ENDLESS LOVE

D SHASHI

Made with <3 on the Notion Press Platform

www.notionpress.com

YOU ARE

You are the sun that rises me
You are the moon that ceases me

You are the pallette I wanna color
You are the poem I wanna write

You are the hug that lights me
You are the kiss that shuts me

You are the cloud that makes me wet
You are the rainbow that brings my
colors out

You are the rain that makes me dance
You are the storm that brings me calm
inside

You are the flower I wanna pluck &
You are the flower I wanna keep safe

You are the beginning that craves me
You are the end that crazes me

EVEN NOW

That song reminded me of you
Even after years

The jewelry gave me that chills
Even after these years

The strawberries tasted like you
Even after these many years

The smoke smelled like you
Even after years

The dreams had your control
Even after these years

The memories still felt alive
Even after these many years

Even my guitar string remembers you
Even after these many years

THE MEMORY

I was the fresher
You were the cool senior

I already fell for you
You were standing high

I gave the interview
You gave me the butterflies

I followed you everywhere
You were on the run

I got your birthday wishes
You got my weird thank you

I saved your pictures
You made my college life

I had you in my dreams
You were living them with her

I have you in my best memories
You are the memory I'll love forever

I'LL BE WAITING FOREVER

I am stuck there
Under those trees
In the red benches
Near that cafe

I crossed that road
Passed those trees
Abandoned those benches
Still found my way back

I promise you
I sweared to myself
That I won't take a U-turn
That i'll be happy for both you and me

But my heart crossed its fingers
Eyes broke the promise
My feet led me there again

At this moment every inch of me betrayed me
At this moment I realized
I'll be waiting forever

JUST FOR YOU

The sweetest dream was you
My bitter truth was also you

The best flashback was you
My worst memory was also you

The daydreams were you
My nightmares were also you

The love I had was you
My hate was also yours

The butterflies were for you
My fears were also for you

The bright skies were you
My dark nights were also you

The rules were broke for you
My heart also broke just for you

JUST SCARED

I am scared of the blacks
Just like I am of the shadows

I am scared of the blues
Just like I am of the dreams

I am scared of the greens
Just like I am of the feelings

I am scared of the reds
Just like I am of the hearts

I am scared of the oranges
Just like I am of the destiny

I am scared of the whites
Just like I am of the tears

I am scared of the colorless
Just like I am of my own heart

REMEMBERING YOU

Remember when you invited me to play
The book I stole from home for you,
Your mom's food, that you shared

Remember when you came over to stay
The math I taught you
The chocolates my mom baked

Remember when I came crying
The worst day it was I said to you
Your shirt wiped my tears, as you cared

Remember when I was leaving
The last puzzle we solved
Your farewell gift I still hold

Remembering you is nostalgia
But not being able to see you
The fear that you don't remember
Makes me think I am a fool
But still those memories are cool

LEAVING

I decided to leave
Before we became indelible

But you didn't leave
I still love that music
I still watch those movies
I still visit those cafes
You were supposed to leave

Thought of leaving was easy
But the thoughts aren't leaving

That song still calms me
That scene still humors me
That waiter still wishes you
Even my dreams visit you

Not just me, but the universe
Makes me feel, your presence

It's part of the memories
Stuck forever, Never leaving

THE KARMA

We flirted, we laughed
We both did like it

You ran, I walked
We both never met

We had the beaches,
We got the hills too

You had the ring,
But I had those big dreams

We kissed, we hugged
We both liked it

You walked, I ran
We both still apart

I got the ring
But now you were far gone

We were so in love
But it had to be someone else.

THE PAINTING

I knew I couldn't finish the painting
I was not capable of the end
I knew for sure no one could change it
I was never capable of the forever

You said you believed me
You said you can wait
You said I was capable
You showed me beauty of that end

I was hopeful
I was grateful
I was trying
I even started to believe myself

My paints parched hoping
My beliefs broke waiting
My heart crashed finding
You cared only for the painting

THE HIDING

Hiding in the sheets
Away from the worries

Hiding in the darkness
Away from myself

Hiding the light
Unable to touch my soul

Hiding the tears
Unable to cross my eyes

Hiding the sorrow
Unable to cross my lips

Hiding in forever
Unable to be known by anyone

THE TRYING

My heart's on fire
My soul's screaming
My body desperate to move

My outside's calm
My inside's not so silent

No one knows what it is
No one knows what it needs
No one knows that it's me

No door to escape
No window to jump
No exit to be seen

I am striving to think
I am escaping to books
I am feeling to music

I am screaming
No one can see me trying
Not even me myself

EVERYTHING

You love me
Loved my love
Loved my pain too

You loved me
Loved my dreams
Loved my nightmares too

You loved me
Loved my peace
Loved my drama too

You loved me
Loved my texts
Loved my rants too

You loved me
Loved my perfume
Loved my sweat too

You loved me
Loved my everything
Loved me anyways

CHOSE ME

You promised me the sunrise
Sun rose but without you by my side

You made me pancakes
Chocolaty, but without you by my side

You asked me forgiveness
I did and yet you dare miss the sunset

You were the same, breaking the promises
I was the same, each day breaking a little bit more

One day I promised the sunrise for myself
Sun rose just for me

I made myself pancakes too
Chocolaty enough like my freedom

You were the same, breaking
I broke enough to rise again

I flyed away from you
With that sun, pancakes and myself

CHAT WITH HEART

Did i say yes?
Did I say you can?
Did I say we can?

You wanna be his
You wanna get hurt
You wanna love

Did I say no?
Did I say you can't ?
Did I say we can't?

Yet you stop
Yet you bleed
Yet you laugh

Did I say yes?
Did I say you should?
Did I say we should ?

You want his love
You want his hate
You want it all

SHY BY HEART

You weren't shy in the dark but
We were unknown in the light

You weren't shy in the shadows but
We were nemesis in the sun

You weren't shy in the sheets but
We were just parallels on the road

You weren't shy in the dates but
We were unknown in the wedding

You weren't shy in those letters but
We were the ocean and the shore

You weren't shy in those texts but
We were just friends in the cafe

You weren't shy in those jokes but
We were just a joke in the real

You weren't shy by the soul
You were shy BUT by that heart of yours

SHE

I found her
I saw her play
I loved her smile
I admired her talk

She felt like a moon
A flower that smiles
A bird that flys
A wave that's unbound

I couldn't look at the pain behind
I wasn't in her cries
I didn't feel the scars
I was not worth it

She was with me
But she never was with me
We were like the sky and the clouds

The sky doesn't feel their pain
Until the clouds rain

CAN'T CHOOSE YOU

I hate you, I love you
I hate it that I love you too

Stake through my heart
I still can't choose you

Feed me the vervain
I still can't choose you

Rush the cure down my throat
I still can't choose you

Dagger me for a century
I still can't choose you

Seal me in the tomb
I still can't choose you

Trap my soul on the other side
I still can't choose you

I love u both & I hate it too
Maybe I'll be reborn and know